McGuffey's Primer
REVISED VERSION

FLASHCARDS
HELPS
&
HINTS

McGuffey's Primer
Flash Cards, Helps & Hints
A Practical Guide to understanding the 19th century mind

By

Sherry K. Hayes

Copyright August 2012

Visit my blogs: **Large Family Mothering**, *www.ladyofvirtue.blogspot.com*
and
Homeschool Sanity, *www.mcguffeysworld.blogspot.com*.

Contents
(Continued)

Introduction ---------------------------------- 3

Fun Forms ---------------------------- 12-20

Teaching
Reading Tips ---------------------------- 21-24

Games &
Activities ---------------------------------- 25

McGuffey
Flash Cards ---------------------------- 26-34

Short Vowel
Chart ------------------------------------- 35

Sounds
Practice ---------------------------------- 36

Writing
Practice ---------------------------- 37-52

Flash Cards for
each Lesson ------------------------- 53-104

Four Free
Resources ---------------------------------- 104

Introduction

I'm just like every other homeschooling mother; I want the best for my children. I really want them to learn the basics; reading, writing and ciphering. I also want them to learn about life and to be prepared for the demands that will be placed on their intellect while they traverse the turbid waters of a world system at odds with their Creator.

Most importantly, I want to impart to them their great need for a Savior, and the debt they owe to God who would forgive them and call them by His wonderful mercy and grace. Even if they don't take those initial steps to make Christ their own, it's my greatest desire to help lay a foundation that cannot be easily ignored, no matter how hard they may try to run from it or try and drown it out with the noise of the world or other self-interests.

I'm afraid I didn't quite know how to go about things when I first started. I was under the impression that our Greek style of educational instruction was the only one. It was with this misunderstanding that I began my homeschooling journey.

I've tried all types of methods and various curricula, in addition to having a predisposition towards "un-schooling." I've examined the rationale from every school of thought on education, from John Holt, to his arch nemesis, B.F. Skinner (mostly to discover just how inhuman and anti-Christian he was), and from Charlotte Mason and her host of admirers, to the famous public schooling critic John Taylor Gatto, to Mary Pride with her pioneering courage, and almost every other modern author in-between.

I ultimately came to understand what education was *not*, and I had an inkling of what education *could be*, but I was at a loss as to how to put it all together, especially with a group of my own children that were prone to distracted creativity (a tendency they no doubt acquired from me).

Eventually, I began to glimpse into the past; before intellectual theory began to mystify and obfuscate the simplicity of authentic education.

I'm greatly indebted here to the research and analysis of John Taylor Gatto, from whom I learned that Americans were amazingly literate long before the insertion of the "Prussian Method" of schooling.

While it may be true that children of pioneering families struggled to learn to read and write, it's also true that they carried within themselves a drive to learn, and were willing to go to great lengths to acquire basic skills.

(Pictured left), The Great and Small English Letters and Syllables for Children found in *The New England Primer.*

It was amazing to me to uncover that novels I find difficult to read and understand were best-sellers and sold copies well into the millions during this period. If education was so paltry, how did we turn out men and women of such distinctive genius that caused the world to take such notice? And how did this intellectual brilliance surface alongside a high regard for the Bible, traditional morality, and Christianity which was found in every sector of society, from the rural farmer to the venerable legislator?

One great source of education that shaped the minds of the progeny of the original thirteen colonies was the *New England Primer*. This diminutive book was the primary volume for the instruction of reading and writing the better part of the 18th and 19th centuries.

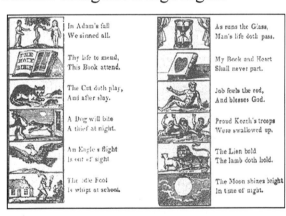

In this small manuscript are contained the bare essentials of the early English alphabet, many lists of words from the simple through to the complex, some prayers and maxims for reading practice and copy work, and even, to its credit, the inclusion of the *Shorter Westminster Catechism*.

It was expected and even understood that the instruction of the young should consist of training in religion and moral responsibility, and in particular, that the whole reason for learning was to grow in "wisdom and stature," and the fear of God being the beginning, the means, and the end of a proper education.

Sherry K. Hayes--Large Family Mothering--www.ladyofvirtue.blogspot.com

Instead of producing generations of biased Pharisees, these books trained the young minds of a new nation in Biblical ethics; with a knowledge of the God-given inalienable rights of each human being. It helped to shape a society in which man's highest goal was to be transformed, by faith and selfless living, into the image of Christ, God's only begotten Son and Savior of the world.

The reason this book was so popular was that it wasn't copy-written, which made it possible to be printed and distributed locally. This meant that the extra costs and difficulties associated with the transporting of these school books were eliminated, making the actual price affordable to all. It was user-friendly and self-explanatory. During a period when almost every child was taught to read at home before entering school (that is, if they decided to attend a formal school at all) parents appreciated the Primer's simplicity and ease of use (you can still buy new copies of this book from numerous sources--I recommend obtaining a copy--my children love it).

As our country became more settled, more highly developed readers were demanded and numerous publishing houses took up the new commission.

William Holmes McGuffey

This is when *William Holmes McGuffey* entered the picture. The eldest son of an Indian scout who emigrated from Scotland to America at the tender age of six, William received his initial formal schooling because of prayer. An itinerate minister was riding past the McGuffey home (the sound of his horse's hooves were muffled by the soft soil so that his presence was undetected) and he overheard the loud supplication of William's mother as she petitioned God for the education of her two sons. This clergyman was so moved that he became a large part of the answer to this mother's heart-felt prayer and before long made arrangements for William's room and board at the "Old Stone Academy." As a consequence of his hard work and acts of Providence, McGuffey went on to become a college professor and faculty member, and at one point even working through college by teaching school. He was also a licensed minister of the Presbyterian Church. His first readers especially reflect a deep abiding faith and have an Evangelistic tone.

McGuffey didn't create a transcript and petition a publisher, the publisher sought him out and requested that this accomplished teacher, speaker, and Christian minister create a series of readers fit for a new, free nation desirous of becoming more moral, noble and patriotic than the world had ever seen.

His first readers were published in 1837, and underwent a number of revisions, many of them carrying the spirit of McGuffey, but with enough additions and exclusions that the end products bore only a resemblance of the original.

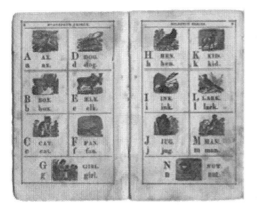

All of the different versions of the *McGuffey Reader Series* sold in the millions of copies. Passages from these books were widely quoted in the publications of the times, by politicians, and even used by foreigners to learn proper English.

Homeschoolers have been rediscovering these outstanding series of books for more than 30 years, and we are presently quite blessed because numerous publishing houses, due to demand, have seen fit to republished both the original and the revised editions of the *McGuffey Reader Series*.

The "digital age" has helped to make it possible for us to benefit from these treasures thanks to entities such as *The Gutenberg Project, Google Books, etc.* Not only do we have the McGuffey's available by the click of a mouse button, but also available are several other analogous reading series which were published during the 19th and early 20th centuries.

It's never been simpler to bless one's children with these resources. They can be read from your computer screen, on an *eReader*, printed out and bound by a local or remote printer, or copies bought from a publisher already bound.

As for the revised McGuffey Primer, any of these methods will produce a book that can be enjoyed by parent and child alike. I personally own two hard copies of this book; one unique set that I accidentally ordered from an antique shop that was originally printed in 1919 (the children aren't allowed to touch this collection!) and one for daily use.

In printing these old books, I select the "two-to-a-page" option in my printer menu dialog box (it sometimes takes a bit of searching for this option, and I have to manually set the page orientation to "landscape" instead of "portrait").

I print out the entire book, but I limit my request to about 20 pages at a time in the printer queue--*because my printer can be rather finicky!* I then use a paper cutter (these are much more available due to the demand for scrapbooking) to cut each page down the middle, arrange them in numerical order, then create covers on cardstock, with plastic for protection, and a large binder clip to hold everything together for the trip to Home Depot's printing and binding services.

I also own the original series offered by Mott Media, and I've enjoyed using these with two of my daughters, one from the very beginning. The guide by Ruth Beechick was very helpful to me, as was the manual by Charles and Betty Burger (it's out of print, but still available for purchase as a used book).

I asked myself just how someone in the 19th century would have used these books; there is almost no instruction included. Especially with the primer, if I hadn't taught reading before, I would have been entirely at a loss!

It was a great boon, then, when I discovered the *Manual of Methods,* which gave me a window into the 19th century mind. For instance, it's in the Manual of Methods that I found descriptions of how to teach reading, long before all of the pedagogy of these present times. Here are a few enlightening quotes:

...The Alphabet, Phonic, Phonetic, Word, or Script methods, and perhaps others, --all have their warm adherents,...and yet we know that almost equally good results are obtained by teachers who use different methods.

No doubt some methods are better than others, and it is certain that some one well-approved method should be adopted; but we wish to warn the young teacher especially of the danger that the method will become a hobby unless he is careful, and that thus the end will be lost sight of in attention to the means. Select your method, and be consistent in its use, but do not allow yourself to be bound by laws that will admit of no display of judgment.

Probably the three most clearly defined and distinctly different methods are the Alphabet, the Word, and the Phonic methods. The Alphabet Method is still used in some of the best graded schools in the country; therefore, the Revised Eclectic Primer and Readers are so prepared as to meet fully the requirements of this method, should a teacher see fit to employ it...By this method, the child is first taught the letters, then to combine the letters into words, and finally to combine words into sentences. No attention is paid in this method to diacritical marks; and the names of letters are taught, not the sounds.

The Word Method teaches a child to recognize words as wholes; and, where objects are used in illustrating the first steps, it is sometimes called the Object Method. This method pays no attention to elementary sounds and diacritical marks. After a number of words are taught as wholes, the children are told the names of the letters and learn to spell.

By the Phonic Method, the child is first taught the elementary sounds of letters; he is then taught to combine these elementary sounds into words. The sound is first taught, and then the character which represents it; the spoken word is learned, and then its written and printed form. This method pays no attention to words as wholes until the elementary sounds composing them are learned.

The Combined Word and Phonic Method first presents the word as a whole, and after a number of words are learned in this way, the elementary sounds composing them are taught, with the characters which represent them.

While McGuffey's Readers are prepared to meet the demands of each of the recognized methods, they are especially adapted to the Phonic Method and to the Combined Word and, which are the two methods most extensively used by successful teachers of primary reading. It is suggested, therefore, that the teacher select one of these methods of instruction. In order that both may be fully understood, we give a rather full description of their different principles and processes.

The Combined Method aims to teach the child to read just as he learned to talk. The child, before coming to school, has learned to associate the spoken word with the object, quality, action, etc., which that word represents. He knows nothing of the component parts of a word; he simply knows the sound of the word as a whole. The Combined Method aims to continue the child's mental development naturally from this point; it utilizes the child's knowledge of the spoken symbol to teach him to associate the corresponding written or printed symbol with the object, quality, or action represented by it.

The Combined Method contemplates the following steps:

1. The object, or picture of the object, is first presented to the child, and its name called for; then the word is given, and written upon the board. Both object and word are observed until the child instantly associates the one with the other.

2. The word is impressed on the child's mind by requiring him to write it, or to print and write it, over and over again.

3. Words united into phrases and sentences are taught in the same manner as single words; that is, the idea is developed first. The child is led to express the thought in words, and these words are then presented to his eye and impressed upon his memory.

4. The child learns the letters or combinations of them himself into phrases and sentences.

5. Words are analyzed, or separated into their elementary sounds.

6. The child learns the letters or combinations of letters that represent these elementary sounds.

7. The child learns to combine the letters so as to form new words.

8. The use of diacritical marks and of the marks of punctuation are learned gradually by the association of ideas.

9. Spelling is unconsciously learned by repeatedly writing the words of the reading lesson.

The other plans for teaching reading are explained still further in the entire text, but I have purposely included only the combined method because this is the more natural and effective of each presented, in my humble opinion.

Specific instructions are included, which might be worth one's effort to read!

Sherry K. Hayes--Large Family Mothering--*www.ladyofvirtue.blogspot.com*

I'm including here pages of tips for using these readers, in a simple form which should be easy for a busy mom (like me) to peruse at a glance so as to encourage and direct. I know from experience with the raising of my own 15 children how chaotic a day can get, and just how many hats a mother must wear. It's good to have a few things at hand as "refreshers" in something like reading instruction, and so I created a few tools that I have found very helpful --*I only wish they were available when I was starting out.*

I've been a great fan of the book, *Teach Your Child to Read in 100 Easy Lessons*, which is an excellent way to begin to understand some of the basics of reading instruction. A beginning homeschooling mother may benefit from the use of this type of book because--*the teacher is instructed.*

But if a person were to start from scratch, it would be very possible to glean the basic ideas from the above mentioned book because they are so easy to understand and to put into practice.

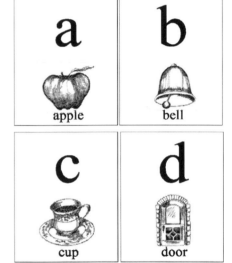

First of all, a child must be taught to read from left-to-right by moving his/her finger under the letters from left-to-right.

Secondly, a child needs to learn to sound out each letter separately and slowly, then combine them slowly, and finally quickly when they become more familiar with them.

These basic methods aren't new and can easily be done no matter what book is being used.

I am including a set of phonics flash cards as well. I've always started with my own children by drilling the basic letter "sounds" and thinking up all kinds of activities to *memorize the sounds* before the letter names are ever learned.

It's my suggestion that the letters and their sound pictures be introduced and memorized first; "a, apple, b, bell," so on and so forth (be careful not to say the "buh" sound, but a staccato "b" so that when a child begins to spell he doesn't automatically add an extra "u" after each hard consonant!).

After the child feels very comfortable with the sounds, and can say them alone without prompting even if they are out-of-order, I recommend the pictures be hidden and the child be required to recite the letter sound after viewing the letter *only*. It's much easier to proceed with reading instruction if these sounds are memorized. There's no time expectation for this exercise--it depends on the child and the amount of time and consistency spent on this practice enterprise. Remember every child is unique.

It's of the utmost importance for the homeschooling mother to remember to keep things fun and maintain a relaxed attitude. A child who feels pressured will not do as well. Furthermore, creating an atmosphere of success will help to sustain your child's interest and keep him from associating learning with drudgery! I've included suggestions along these lines to aid in your young learner's progress.

I'm including some pages of copy work to show just how such a thing could be accomplished. My dear Faith and I are simply using a composition book from *Roaring Springs* to do our copy work. I write it out carefully for her, and then she copies it.

She draws a little box where there is space and creates her own illustration for each lesson. I would recommend the more homey approach of copying the words by hand over the machine-made; *it keeps things more personal coming from the loving heart of a mother to the heart of her child.*

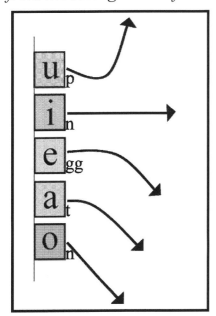

I've created a chart for emphasizing the short vowel sounds (left). All my children have had some trouble differentiating between the short sounds of "e" and "i," so I came up with a way of showing them how each one is different by moving a finger along the arrows drawn as the letter is voiced. It truly helped them, especially when it came to spelling. We practice this over and over, reviewing each and every day before doing anything else, until any pronunciation problems are successfully work out.

There's also a page of syllables to practice these short vowels in the order as they are presented on the chart. The flash cards for the lessons can be used as actual flash cards or printed as posters. One dear mother I read about put posters like these on her child's bed so they could review them together at bedtime.

This method's not a workbook-type plan, where everything is spelled out and programmed. This is meant to be open-ended, requiring more participation on the part of the teacher, but building a better foundation of understanding for the student and thus allowing the teacher to more closely tailor the instruction to the child's specific needs. It's important to know that not every flash card need be used, creative experimentation is an integral part of the learning process.

I've made these helps for the busy mother that doesn't have a lot of time to read and prepare. I hope they will bless you, and help you to feel confident, successful and free to love learning together along with your children.

Fun Booklets

Instead of filling in empty workbooks, why not create original books? This is a great way to encourage young scholarship as soon as a child shows interest and is capable of writing. This can be done along with the lessons, or in lieu of them when a plateau is reached or just when creativity needs to be expressed. Marilyn Howshall the author of *Lifestyle of Learning* recommends these for young children.

I have created templates with a number of ideas, and a blank one for original stories and other types, such as:

My Dog, Cat, etc.
My Favorite Flowers
My Favorite Foods
My Numbers
A Happy Day
God's Flood
Our Vacation
Original story titles, etc.

Just print and fill out the front page, and then as many of the inner pages as necessary. You can print them full-page size, or half page. They can be stapled together, put in a three-ring binder, or even comb or spiral bound (there are even ways to sew the pages together).

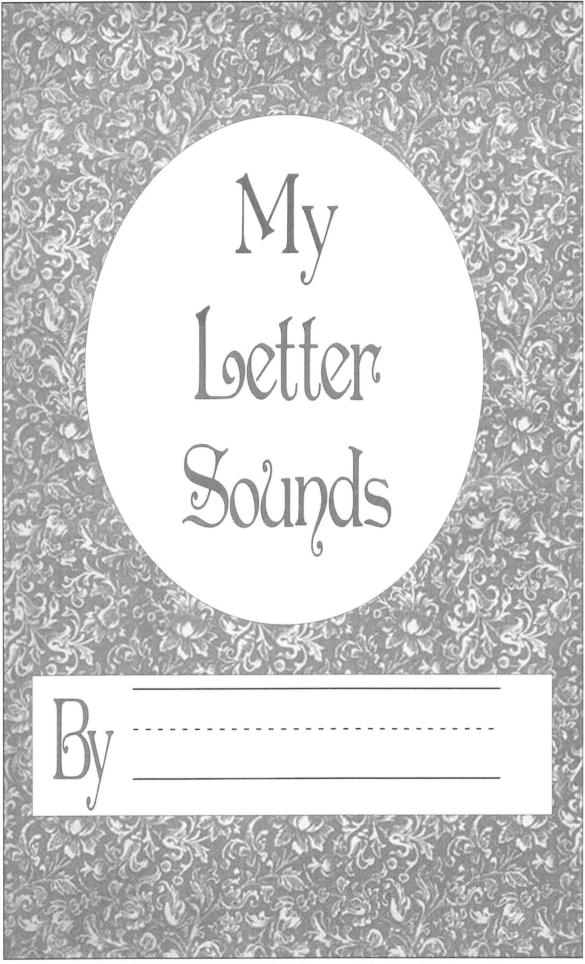

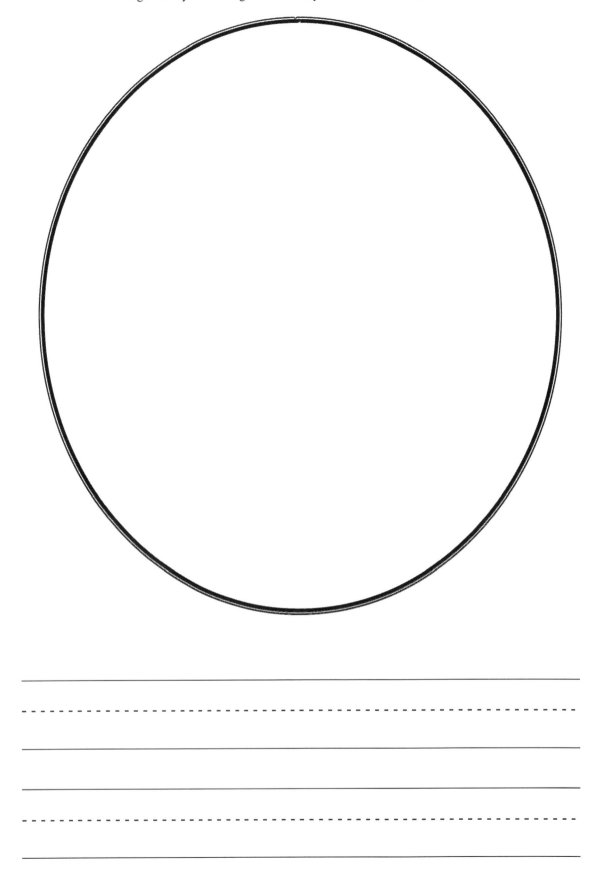

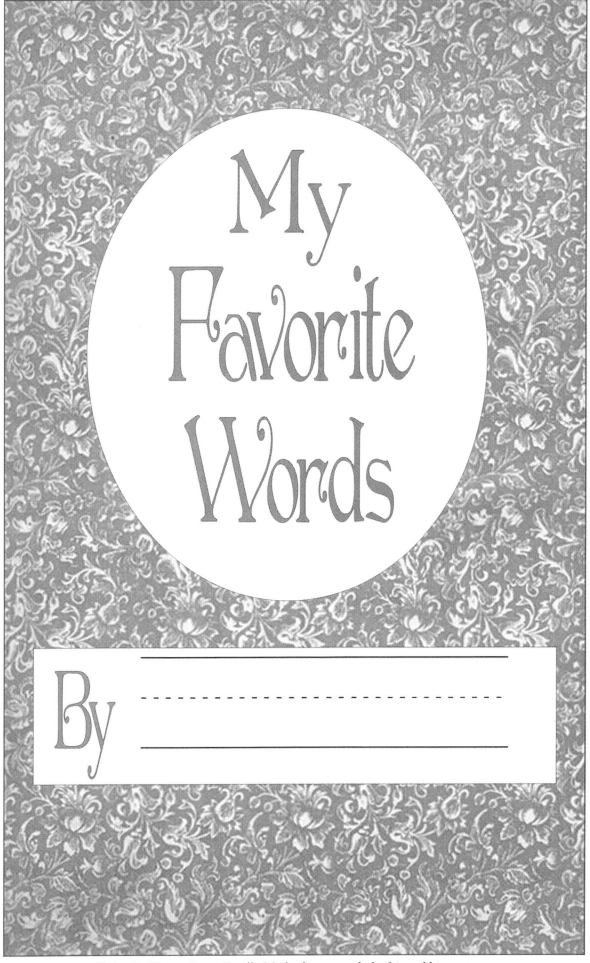

Teaching Reading TIPS

Keep it fun!

"We **get** to," *not*, "we **have** to."   Learn to quit *before* frustration sets in.

Keep it special!

Snuggle close--on a couch if it is available.

Keep some supplies, such as crayons, pencils, copybooks, etc. separate and designated only for "learning time."

Set the stage by getting the wiggles out--*dancing to music, going for a walk, etc., and picking a quiet time.*

Offer a non-messy snack such as some cheese crackers, craisins or banana chips--*little children have a hard time concentrating if they are hungry.* You are creating memories that will help your child think of learning as a pleasant activity.

Keep it short and sweet!

Study no more than 15-20 minutes at a time, four or five times a week.

Consistency is more important than intensity.

For most children, progress will be gradual. Don't allow yourself to become worried because your child is not learning as fast as you expect. If you do, you will be tempted to cram, creating a stressful environment that will backfire in the long run.

Sherry K. Hayes--Large Family Mothering--*www.ladyofvirtue.blogspot.com*

Start with reading.

Read aloud--*follow the words with your fingers.*

Have lots of books around for the child to enjoy. Start with library books, then collect books for your own library than can be read over and over.

Teach the sounds.

Teach the sounds before you teach the alphabet.

Don't say "buh," say, "b"--*there is a great difference when a child goes to spell a word from its sound.*

Simply go through your phonics flash cards once a day for a number of days. Then begin to use different games to check for mastery.

Use the short vowel chart to help the child properly differentiate between the short vowel sounds. It's arranged in a specific order--the way a child's mouth should move with each sound--*up, straight, down slightly, and so on.* This should be reviewed daily until mastered. The syllable chart can be used for further practice.

Sound it out.

Voice each letter separately, from left to right, moving your finger underneath as you go.

Say the sounds together slowly, and then quickly. Have the child do the same until smooth.

Repeat until mastered.

It is perfectly OK to stay on the same lesson for a couple of weeks.

Begin by reading it aloud for your child,
then have him read it with you, then by himself.

Use the words both in and out of context. Children learn more easily
when the words are in actual sentences than just out of thin air.
The flash cards are only to reinforce what is contained in the lesson.

The more familiar we are with any subject matter, the more relaxed
and confident we become. This is the goal of these primer lessons;
to allow a child to become familiar with words.

Time out for maturity

A lot of reading requires visual memory. Some children do not develop
the capacity for fine visual memorization until seven, eight or even as old
as 14 years of age! It is hard to be patient, but oftentimes when students
are forced too early, their interest wanes, and their inability to read
on their own intuitively may be prolonged.

Study your child to determine whether he is simply lazy, or actually fatigued
by the exercises. Whenever I sense frustration, we instantly stop and do
something light. I say, "Learning time is fun time, so let's give this up and
have some fun!" I then offer up a snack or some special craft or play time--the
frowns usually turn to smiles as the feelings of pressure are relieved.

Plenty of time for "free play" is a great way to allow a child to mature for
reading. Open-ended toys, such as blocks, Lego's, etc. are the best.

Make it interesting.

Play games with each lesson (use the list provided as a bookmark to remind you of different activities).

Give it a break.

Give seasons of rest along with a season of consistent lessons. Young children need to be able to mature in their spiritual, mental, emotional and physical selves in order to learn well. As stated previously, playing and discovery go a long way towards learning to read.

Use discussion.

Use the pictures to encourage discussion, even story telling. Spend the first part of each lesson allowing the child to express his different observations to you--give him your whole attention and enjoy this time getting to know who he is and how he thinks. Appeal to this as you are using the lesson.

Use whole words and context.

Be careful not to over-correct. If a child is guessing words from context, allow it. If you wait a while, he may even correct himself when he realizes what he reads doesn't make sense or just doesn't sound right.

Use creativity.

Some children like to draw, some like to sing, others like to create in 3-D with Legos, Play Dough, etc. They can draw and create anything suggested in the lesson or the pictures.

Games & Activities

ABC Train: Arrange the phonics cards into alphabetical order on the table or floor. Sing the ABC song as you point to each card or pick it up. You could put the word and sound flash cards in alphabetical order.

Find it: Place a number of cards on the table. Name a sound and have the child find it. He can keep every card he identifies correctly.

Notebook it: This can be done with the ABC's or words for the lessons. Each page of a notebook/composition book can be dedicated to a different sound or word, with cutouts from magazines or original drawings.

Stump the student: Have the child give you a spelling test--spell a few wrong and see if he can catch it--always fun!

Goofy story time: Use the words in the lesson to make up a silly story. Draw a picture to go with it.

Find the word: Call out a word and have the child find it in the lesson. You could have the child pick a card at random from the deck of flash cards to find in the lesson.

Spell it: Pick out words at random and have the child spell them out loud, or, better yet, write them (allow him to peek if he gets stuck--keep it fun!).

a

apple

b

bell

c

cup

d

door

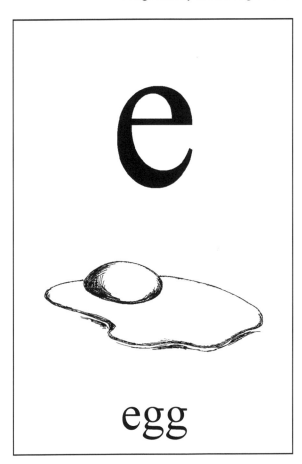
egg

fish

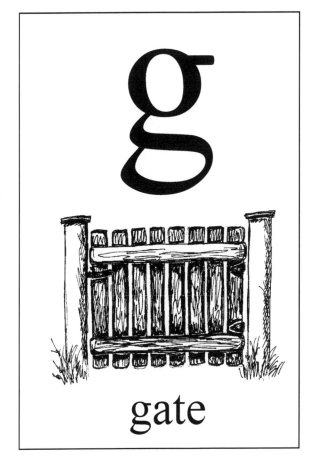
gate

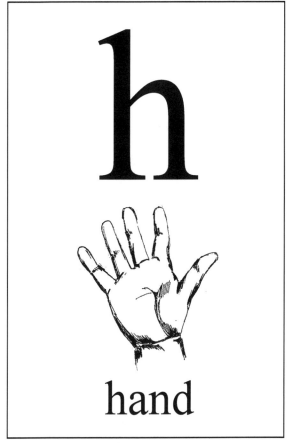
hand

igloo

jar

kite

lamp

m

moon

n

nut

o

octopus

p

pie

q

quail

r

rake

s

sunflower

t

teapot

u

umbrella

v

vase

w

window

x

ax

y

yoyo

z

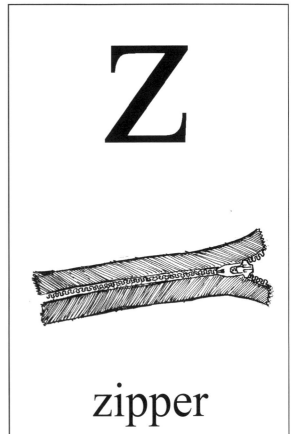

zipper

ā

acorn

ē

eagle

ī
ice cream

ō
overalls

ū
ukulele

ch
cherries

sh

shoe

th

thimble

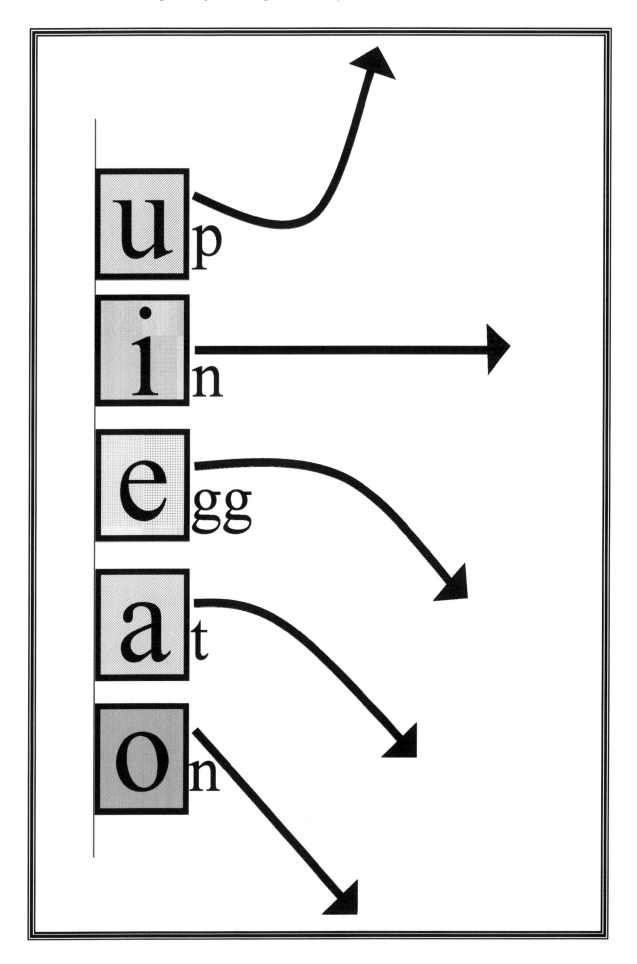

Sounds Practice

Bu	bi	be	ba	bo
Du	di	de	da	do
Fu	fi	fe	fa	fo
Gu	gi	ge	ga	go
Hu	hi	he	ha	ho
Ju	ji	je	ja	jo
Ku	ki	ke	ka	ko
Lu	li	le	la	lo
Mu	mi	me	ma	mo
Nu	ni	ne	na	no
Pu	pi	pe	pa	po
Ru	ri	re	ra	ro
Su	si	se	sa	so
Tu	ti	te	ta	to
Vu	vi	ve	va	vo
Wu	wi	we	wa	wo

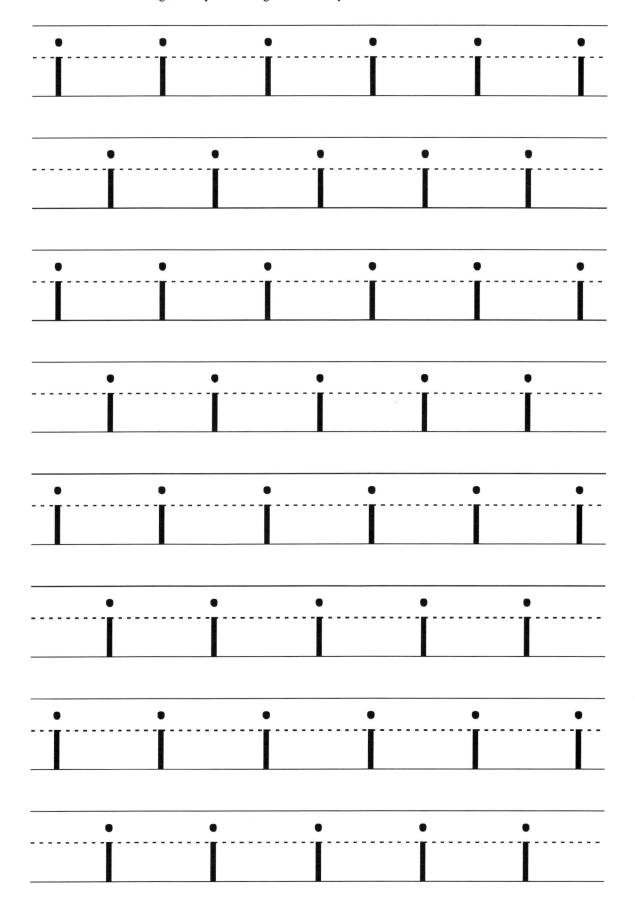

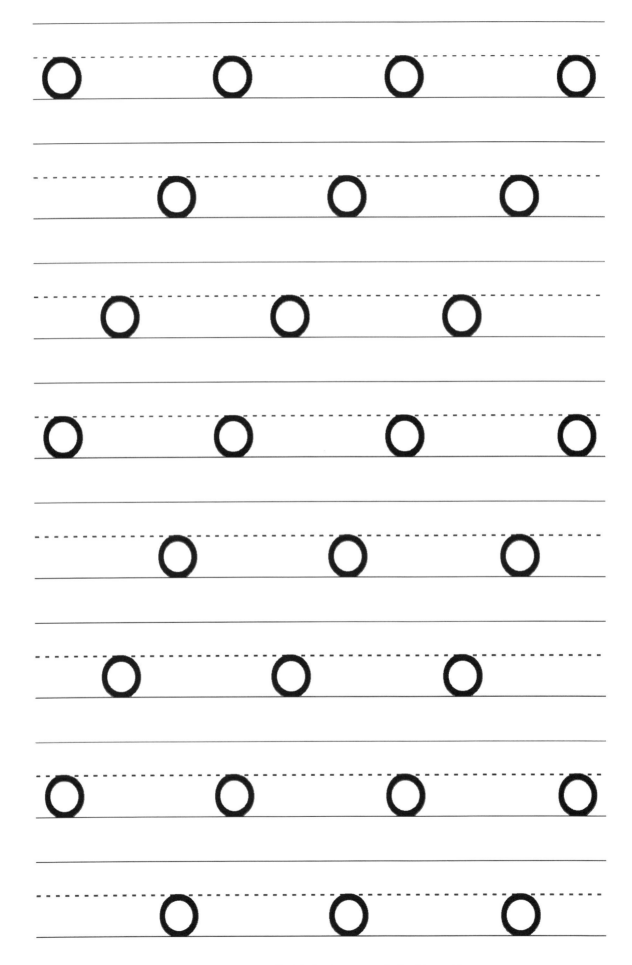

A rat a rat

A cat a cat

A rat a rat

A cat a cat

A rat and a cat

The cat has a rat.
Ann has a hat

Ann and Nat

Ann can fan

Nat.

A man and

a lad.

Ann has a hat and a fan.

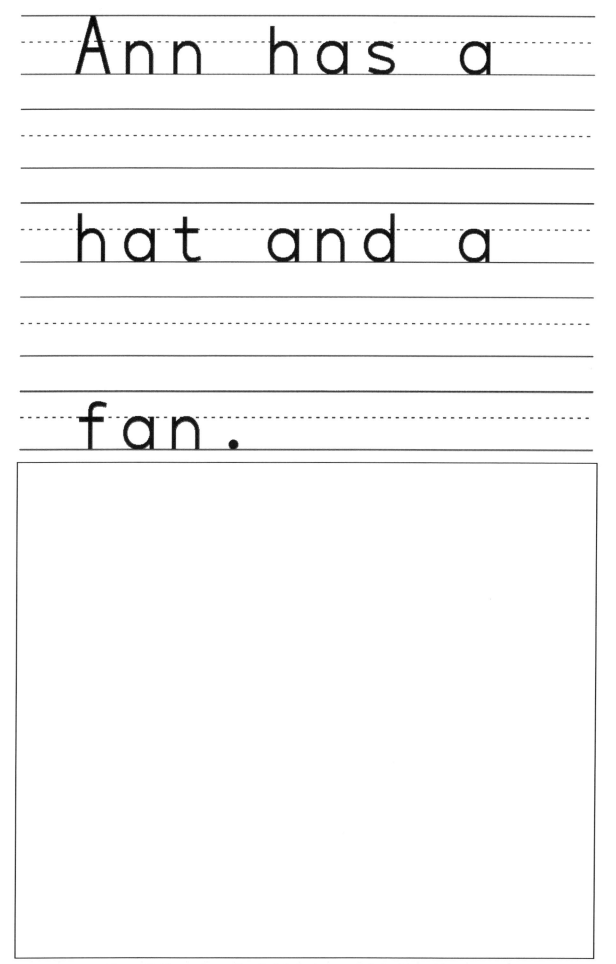

The lad has

a fat dog.

See the frog on the log.

The lamp is

Nat's, and

the mat is

Ann's.

Can Tom

catch his

nag?

Nat's dog,

Rab, can not

catch the

rat.

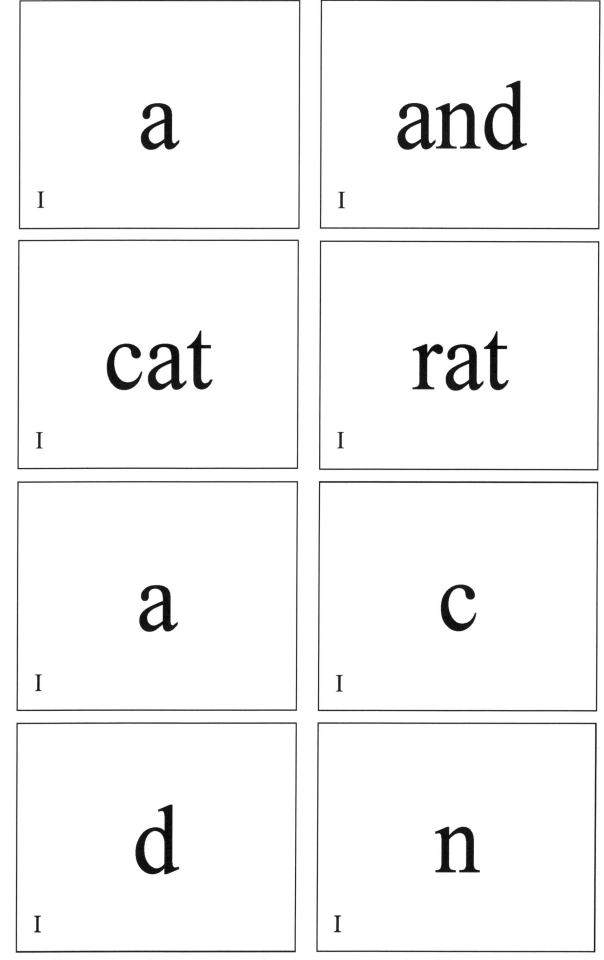

r

t

a rat

a cat

A cat

A rat

at	the
ran	has
Ann	h
th	s

Nat — III	hat — III
fan — III	can — III
f — III	a fan — III
a hat — III	II

man	cap
IV	IV

lad	sat
IV	IV

l	m
IV	IV

p	s
IV	IV

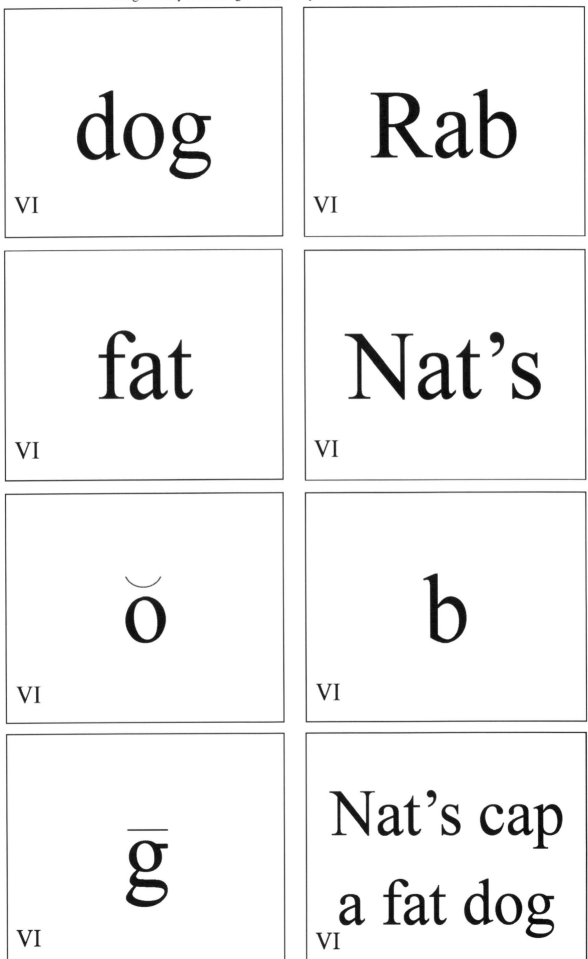

see	sees
VII	VII

frog	on
VII	VII

log	ē
VII	VII

A log	the frog
VII	VII

it VIII	stand VIII
Ann's VIII	is VIII
lamp VIII	mat VIII
ĭ VIII	a mat / the stand VIII

Tom

nag

not

him

catch

he

his

ch

nest	this
XI	XI
eggs	she
XI	XI
in	get
XI	XI
box	hen
XI	XI

e XI	x XI
sh XI	the box a nest XI
old XII	run XII
fox XII	ō XII

e XI	x XI
sh XI	the box a nest XI
old XII	run XII
fox XII	ō XII

ŭ	pond
XII	XIII

ducks	them
XIII	XIII

feed	Nell
XIII	XIII

I	by
XIII	XIII

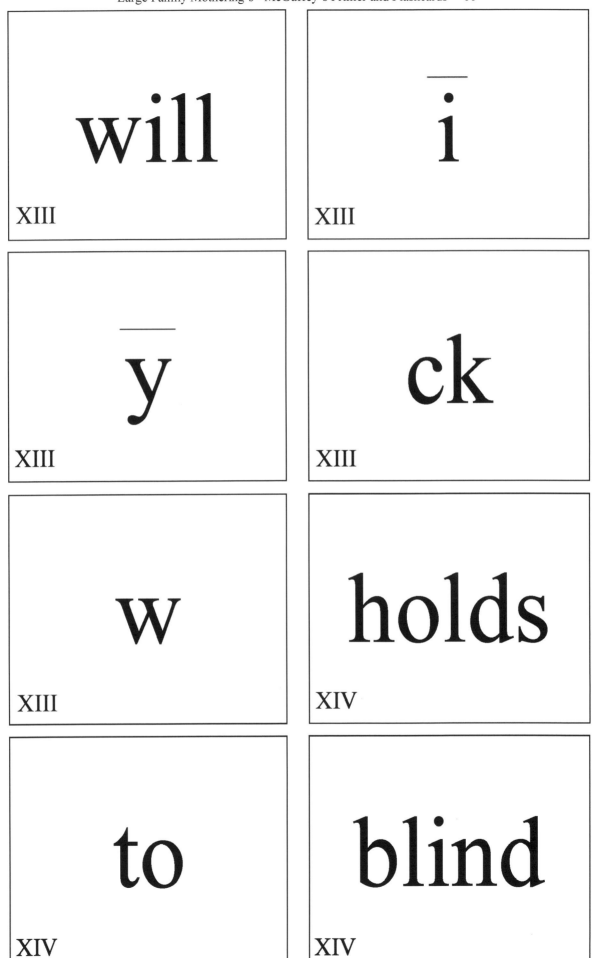

Mary XIV	**hand** XIV
kind XIV	**ā** XIV
o̤ XIV	**k** XIV
y̆ XIV	**Sue** XVI

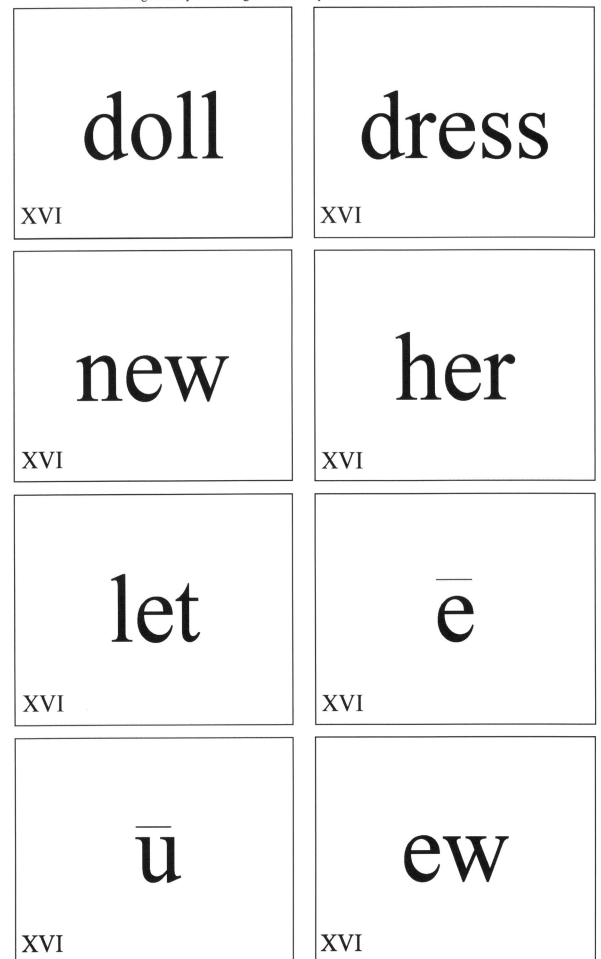

there	five
XVII	XVII

bird	tree
XVII	XVII

rob	do
XVII	XVII

ẽ	ĩ
XVII	XVII

v XVII	cage XVIII
pet XVIII	sing XVIII
lives XVIII	so XVIII
loves XVIII	ȯ XVIII

boys XIX	**of** XIX
play XIX	**what** XXI
owl XXI	**an** XXI
well XXI	**eyes** XXI

night	day
XXII	XXII
but	big
XXII	XXII
best	ạ
XXII	XXII
ow	wh
XXII	XXII

grass XXII	they XXII
come XXII	off XXII
barn XXII	shade XXII
hot XXII	cows XXII

our	e
XXII	XXII

ou	soon
XXII	XXIII

sun	neck
XXIII	XXIII

set	way
XXIII	XXIII

bell XXIII	**one** XXIII
their XXIII	**ōō** XXIII
brave XXIV	**if** XXIV
ship XXIV	**boat** XXIV

drown XXIV	**men** XXIV
rock XXIV	**save** XXIV
fall XXVI	**ice** XXVI
skates XXVI	**cry** XXVI

with	had
XXVI	XXVI
stone	did
XXVI	XXVI
ä	ç
XXVI	XXVI
sk	look
XXVI	XXVI

go — XXVII	John — XXVII
here — XXVII	all — XXVII
wheel — XXVII	mill — XXVII
have — XXVII	round — XXVII

oŏ XXVII	j XXVII
or XXVIII	Jane XXVIII
girls XXVIII	floor XXVIII
roll XXVIII	some XXVIII

which XXVIII	**black** XXVIII
ô XXVIII	**for** XXIX
out XXIX	**as** XXIX
how XXIX	**try** XXIX

horse XXIX	should XXIX
hurt XXIX	cars XXIX
be XXIX	$\underset{.}{o}$ XXIX
no XXIX	$\hat{u}$ XXIX

work	ax
XXXI	XXXI
pile	Ned
XXXI	XXXI
think	wood
XXXI	XXXI
saw	hard
XXXI	XXXI

cut XXXI	**õ** XXXI
th XXXI	**n̲** XXXI
noise XXXII	**air** XXXII
here XXXII	**gone** XXXII

May XXXII	**walk** XXXII
cool XXXII	**two** XXXII
â XXXII	**oi** XXXII
pull XXXIII	**cart** XXXIII

goats	Bess
XXXIII	XXXIII
up	ride
XXXIII	XXXIII
hill	ŭ
XXXIII	XXXIII
blaze	put
XXXIV	XXXIV

yet XXXIV	house XXXIV
fire XXXIV	roof XXXIV
call XXXIV	ring XXXIV
we XXXIV	z XXXIV

Miss XXXVI	wants XXXVI
would XXXVI	tells XXXVI
rule XXXVI	keep XXXVI
good XXXVI	that XXXVI

each	ü
XXXVI	XXXVI
school	church
XXXVII	XXXVII
books	slates
XXXVII	XXXVII
child	when
XXXVII	XXXVII

quail	seen
XXXVIII	XXXVIII
me	eat
XXXVIII	XXXVIII
know	quick
XXXVIII	XXXVIII
kill	oh
XXXVIII	XXXVIII

first XXXVIII	**Henry** XXXVIII
qu XXXVIII	**Kate** XXXIX
name XXXIX	**baby** XXXIX
shut XXXIX	**dear** XXXIX

blue XXXIX	**near** XXXIX
crib XXXIX	**sit** XXXIX
light XLI	**where** XLI
far XLI	**sea** XLI

its XLI	tall XLI
high XLI	were XLI
wrong XLII	wolf XLII
us XLII	my XLII

took XLII	**sheep** XLII
watch XLII	**more** XLII
lambs XLII	**laugh** XLIII
snow XLIII	**head** XLIII

fun
XLIII

mouth
XLIII

made
XLIII

pipe
XLIII

gh(as f)
XLIII

sweets
XLIV

mean
XLIV

please
XLIV

bee	buzz
XLIV	XLIV
vine	could
XLIV	XLIV
said	once
XLIV	XLIV
while	done
XLVI	XLVI

might XLVI	right XLVI
time XLVI	your XLVI
things XLVI	halves XLVI
went XLVII	fish XLVII

fell XLVII	**safe** XLVII
arms XLVII	**sprang** XLVII
was XLVII	**thank** XLVII
got XLVII	**James** XLVII

then XLVIII	**asks** XLVIII
drives XLVIII	**warm** XLVIII
been XLVIII	**town** XLVIII
show XLVIII	**I'll** XLIX

puss XLIX	pat XLIX
harm XLIX	she'll XLIX
don't XLIX	purr XLIX
furr XLIX	deeds XLIX

now	wreathes
who	queen
woods	shall
crown	God

small	world
shine	long
from	moon
nut	ago

Lord LII	morn LII
smile LII	griefs LII
joys LII	woes LII
tear LII	stars LII

nigh
LII

say
LII

SPECIAL PURCHASE OFFER
FOUR FREE HOMESCHOOL RESOURCES:

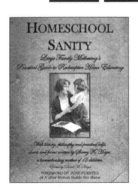

Get yours when you buy the paperback version of Sherry Hayes' new book, "Homeschool Sanity," on *Amazon.com* you will receive the *PDF versions* of *Homeschool Sanity (178 pages)*, *Large Family Mothering's 2012-2013 Homeschool Planner (127 pages)*, *McGuffey's Primer Flashcards and Helps*, and *Ray's Arithmetics Flash Cards & Helps*.

ALL ARE PRINTABLE AND READY FOR BINDING!

OFFER GUIDELINES:

1) Simply send us *Amazon's order verification e-mail* that shows you purchased Sherry's new book, "Homeschool Sanity" or a copy of the packing invoice and then forward it in an e-mail: *largefamilymothering@gmail.com*. Please include the subject line in your e-mail: **Four Free Homeschool Resources**. *That's all there is to it!*

Once your e-mail is received we will send you the absolutely free download link. These four valuable resources normally cost **$27.49!** *You will get them absolutely **FREE!!!***

Homeschool Sanity: *a Practical Guide to Redemptive Home Educating* is Sherry Hayes' attempt to communicate a way back to common sense learning. Rediscover the tools of learning that helped our forefathers overcome great obstacles! Discover a pathway back to the simplicity and joy of gaining the knowledge born out of a reverence for the God of the Bible. **Gain clarity. Find Peace.**

Sherry K. Hayes--Large Family Mothering--*www.ladyofvirtue.blogspot.com*

Printed in Great Britain
by Amazon.co.uk, Ltd.,
Marston Gate.